HITTING
THE
BOOKS
Skills for Reading, Writing, and Research

Library
Skills
and
Internet
Research

Precious McKenzie

Rourke
Educational Media

rourkeeducationalmedia.com

*Scan for Related Titles
and Teacher Resources*

Before Reading:

Building Academic Vocabulary and Background Knowledge

Before reading a book, it is important to tap into what your child or students already know about the topic. This will help them develop their vocabulary, increase their reading comprehension, and make connections across the curriculum.

1. *Look at the cover of the book. What will this book be about?*
2. *What do you already know about the topic?*
3. *Let's study the Table of Contents. What will you learn about in the book's chapters?*
4. *What would you like to learn about this topic? Do you think you might learn about it from this book? Why or why not?*
5. *Use a reading journal to write about your knowledge of this topic. Record what you already know about the topic and what you hope to learn about the topic.*
6. *Read the book.*
7. *In your reading journal, record what you learned about the topic and your response to the book.*
8. *After reading the book complete the activities below.*

Content Area Vocabulary
Read the list. What do these words mean?

access
biased
bibliography
brainstorm
catalog
guide
Internet
keyword
librarian
materials
reliable
research
resources
revise
reword
roadblocks
website

After Reading:

Comprehension and Extension Activity

After reading the book, work on the following questions with your child or students in order to check their level of reading comprehension and content mastery.

1. *Why is the library a good place to gather research for a project? (Asking Questions)*
2. *With thousands of websites to choose from how do you know which ones are best for your project? (Infer)*
3. *What are some things you can do if you run into a roadblock? (Text to self connection)*
4. *How does using the library and Internet help ensure you will gather all the necessary information you need? (Summarize)*
5. *Suppose you have a big project at school and want to research at the library. What would be the first thing you would do? (Visualize)*

Extension Activity

3 4873 00511 8799

Your teacher has assigned a big project that is due in one week. Keep a journal on how you prepared for it, and in what order you did your research. Did you search the Internet first, go to the library and look at printed material, or do a little of both each day? Record your steps in your journal and remember to use them next time you are assigned a project.

Table of Contents

Let's Get Started

What should you do when your teacher assigns a big project? Don't panic. Make a research plan and head to your library. With a plan and the right tools, you will have your project done on time.

Ask yourself questions about your topic before you start to research.

Your teacher probably gave you a topic to **research**, or find more information about. What do you already know about this topic? Your background knowledge can get you started in the right direction. It's a good idea to write that information in your notebook.

What would you like to know about the topic? Before you head to the library, **brainstorm** a list of questions to research. Write those questions in your notebook.

Take your questions with you to the library. Those questions will **guide** your search.

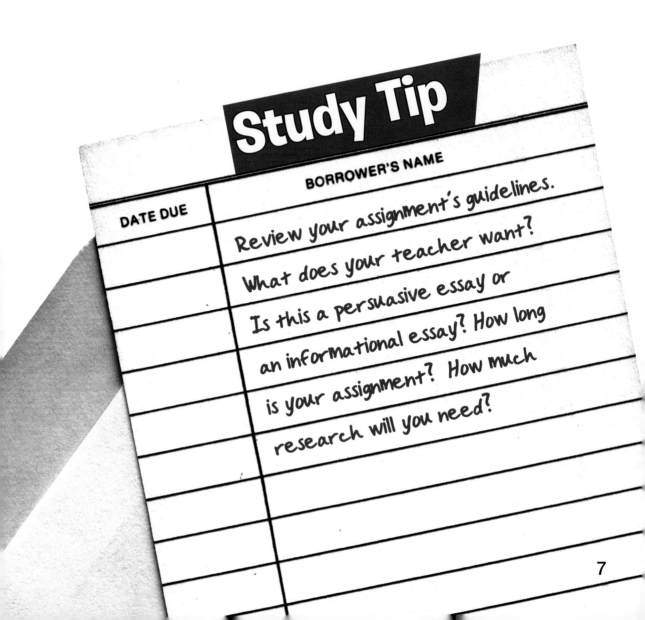

Study Tip

DATE DUE	BORROWER'S NAME
	Review your assignment's guidelines.
	What does your teacher want?
	Is this a persuasive essay or
	an informational essay? How long
	is your assignment? How much
	research will you need?

Library Resources

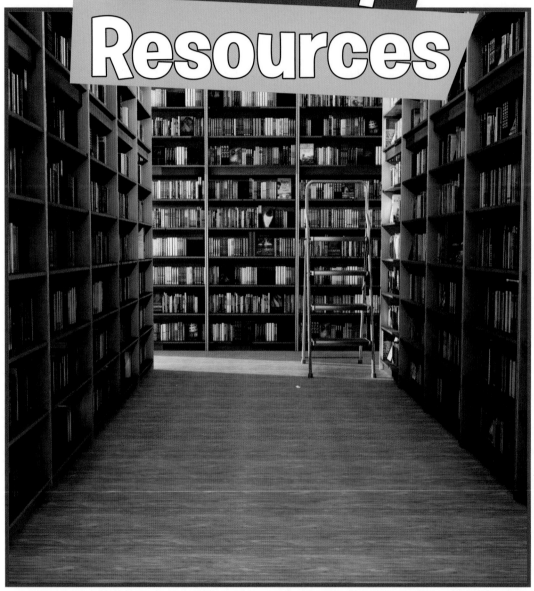

Libraries contain thousands of **resources** in one location. Sometimes it can be overwhelming. That is until you know where to begin.

Most libraries use an electronic **catalog** to keep track of all of their resources. You can log on to the computer and search the library's catalog for more information on your topic. The catalog allows users to search by subject, **keyword**, author, or title.

Give yourself plenty of time in the library to complete your research. You might be surprised at all the fascinating information you will find.

First, type in a keyword that relates to your research project. The catalog will show you a list of **materials** that includes books, ebooks, databases, movies, music, and even audiobooks about your topic. Next, carefully read through the list of results. Which items look like they fit your topic? Create a marked checklist and later track down your sources!

Study Tip

Librarians often suggest that you search by keyword when you are just starting your research. This way you won't accidentally miss possible sources.

If you need to locate library materials, the library catalog will give you important information. The catalog can tell you if the book is checked out. It can also tell you which section of the library has the book or how to **access** the ebook.

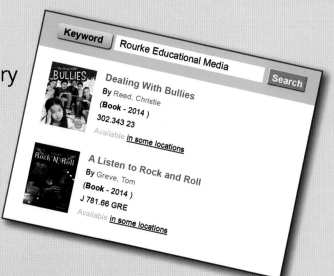

How to Use the Dewey Decimal System	
Numbers	**Categories**
000-099	General References or Works
100-199	Philosophy, Psychology, and Logic
200-299	Religion
300-399	Social Sciences
400-499	Language
500-599	Natural Science
600-699	Technology and Applied Science
700-799	Fine Arts and Recreation
800-899	Literature
900-999	History and Biographies

When you find the books you need you can stay in the library and take notes. Keep careful record of where you find your information. Your teacher will probably want a list of your sources. List the author's name, book title, publisher, place of publication, and year to include in your **bibliography**.

Remember, write your notes and ideas in your research notebook, not in the library books.

You can check books out and return them when you are finished reading them. Many libraries allow you to borrow their materials for up to 28 days! Your **librarian** will help you with checking out and answer all your questions. Some reference materials cannot leave the library. Many encyclopedias, dictionaries, and maps cannot be checked out. But, you can always take notes or make photocopies to take home.

Be a Respectful Library Patron

1. Take care of all library materials so they stay in good shape for many years.
2. Use a quiet voice in the library so other people can concentrate on their studies.
3. Leave your cell phone at home or turned off so you don't disturb others.
4. Clean up your work area before you leave.
5. Place all materials back on carts so they can be reshelved.
6. Your good manners will help to make the library a pleasant and productive place for all the patrons!

Using the Internet

Ask your teacher which search engine to use. Many teachers use Google and Bing.

Besides the library where can you go for more information about your topic? The **Internet**! With just a few keystrokes you will have hundreds of sources in a matter of seconds.

Finding sources on the Internet is similar to searching the library's online catalog. You will type your keywords in the search bar. A list of websites will appear. You can begin reading through the websites or, if there doesn't seem to be any websites with the information you need, you can **reword** your search.

With thousands of websites to choose from, how do you know which ones are better than others? That's a tough question. Good websites have accurate and up to date information. As a researcher, you should only use **reliable** websites.

Is the Site Reliable?

Use this checklist to help you find reliable Internet sources.

1. Is the **website** advertising something?
2. Is the website trying to sell you a product? If you answered "yes," then the website might just be out to make money or the site might be **biased** toward its own product and agenda.
3. Is the author of the website an expert on the topic? Where does he or she work? Does the author have special knowledge or training on the subject matter?
4. Is the content on the website up to date?

When you think you have a reliable source, perform another search. One way to see if the information is reliable is to check it against information on other websites. If the results match up then you've probably found reliable information.

Some websites are not safe. Those websites contain violent or graphic content. Or, the websites might be looking to steal your personal information. Be safe when using the Internet. If you find a sketchy website, tell your teacher right away so she can block the website.

You can also **access** online versions of dictionaries and encyclopedias to help you with your research. These online reference materials contain the same information as the print versions you find in the library and they are just as reliable.

There are several different types of websites. If the web address ends in ".com" it is a commercial or for—profit website. Non—profit websites like ".org" are not out to make a profit. Sites that end in ".gov" belong to the government. Sites that end in ".edu" are education related. Most experts agree that .gov and .edu sites contain accurate facts.

When you find reliable source material on the Internet, you can take notes in your notebook. Or, you can print the websites and write your notes on the printed pages.

Remember to give credit where credit is due. You will need to list the Internet sources you used for any school project.

Overcoming Roadblocks

Sometimes when you perform library and Internet research you can run into **roadblocks**. Maybe you can't find any information at all about your topic. Maybe you're finding too much information. What can you do to solve your problem?

Try to **revise** your search terms. With a keyword search you will have a long list of sources that deal with your topic. You can make your search more specific by searching for more detailed words or phrases. With each new search, different results will appear. Keep searching until you find just what you need.

Research takes time and effort. If you run into a roadblock, ask a librarian or teacher to help you. With a little practice, you'll soon be on your way to success!

Compare Your Results

1. Choose your search engine.
2. Type in the word "dog." What types of websites appear?
3. Now, run a new search. Type in the words "dog names."
4. Analyze the differences between the two searches. What types of information did you find with each search? How might you use the information from either search?

Glossary

access (AK-sess): to get information using a computer

biased (BYE-uhst): showing favor over one point of view more than another

bibliography (bib-lee-OG-ruh-fee): a list of the materials you read about your research topic

brainstorm (BRAYN-storm): to generate ideas quickly

catalog (KAT-uh-log): a list or database of all the books in a library

guide (GIDE): to lead you, or to help you

Internet (IN-tur-net): electronic network of information that you can access through the computer

keyword (KEE-wurd): a specific word you use in a search

librarian (LYE-brer-ee-uhn): a specially trained person who works in a library

materials (muh-TIHR-ee-uhlz): the actual objects that you can find in a library

reliable (ri-LYE-uh-buhl): dependable, accurate, and trustworthy

research (ri-SURCH): to investigate or study

resources (ri-SORSS-iz): valuable sources of information

revise (ri-VYEZ): to redo or change

reword (ri-WURD): to say or write something using different words

roadblocks (ROHD-BLOKSS): barriers

website (WEB-site): a group of linked files on the Internet

Index

Websites to Visit

www.fbi.gov/fun-games/kids/kids-safety

atyourlibrary.org/sixty-ways-use-your-library-card

www.ala.org/aasl/aboutaasl/aaslcommunity/quicklinks/k12students/aaslkctools

About the Author

Precious McKenzie lives in Billings, Montana. She teaches college students how to perform research, take notes, and write really long research papers. In her free time, she likes to read books and ride horses.

Meet The Author!
www.meetREMauthors.com

www.rourkeeducationalmedia.com

PHOTO CREDITS: Cover © visionchina, Goodluz; title page © Cathy Veulet, Susan Kapecky; page 3 © Robyn Mackenzie; page 4 © cocozero003; page 5 © Tyler Olson, page 6 © ariwasabi; page 7, 10 © Angela Farley; page 8 © mikekiev; page 9 © JaniBryson; page 10 © ammentorp; page 11 © Rourke Educational Media; page 12, 20 © Wavebreak Media LTD; page 14, 17 © 3bugsmom, 15 © Cathy Yeulet; page 18 © dolphfyn; page 19 © Syda Productions

Edited by: Jill Sherman

Cover Design by: Tara Raymo

Interior Design by: Jen Thomas

Library of Congress PCN Data

Library Skills and Internet Research / Precious McKenzie
(Hitting the Books: Skills for Reading, Writing, and Research)
ISBN (hard cover) 978-1-62717-687-3 (alk. paper)
ISBN (soft cover) 978-1-62717-809-9
ISBN (e-Book) 978-1-62717-924-9
Library of Congress Control Number: 2014935462

Rourke Educational Media
Printed in the United States of America,
North Mankato, Minnesota

Also Available as: